UNDER A

MEDLAR TREE

T0363539

If love be blind, love cannot hit the mark.
Now will he sit under a medlar tree
And wish his mistress were that kind of fruit
As maids call medlars when they laugh alone.
O, Romeo, that she were, O that she were
An open et cetera, thou a pop'rin pear!

Romeo and Juliet

UNDER A
MEDLAR TREE

Syd Harrex

LYTHRUM PRESS
ADELAIDE

First published by
Lythrum Press
128 Hindley Street
Adelaide
South Australia 5000

June 2004

Cover photograph of a medlar tree by Alan Mayne

Designed and typeset in Giovanni 10/13 by Michael Deves
Printed and bound by Hyde Park Press

ISBN 0 9751260 8 3

Contents

Acknowledgements

I gratefully thank Danni Gray, Katy Hasenohr and Anne Rizzo
for typing original manuscripts;

Nena Bierbaum for professional preparation of the book
for the publisher;

Michael Deves for his publishing expertise and book design;

Judy King for assiduous proof-reading;

Alan Mayne for the cover photograph of the medlar tree in
Judy and Alan's garden in rural Victoria;

the family of David Harrex for permission to reproduce the painting
on the back cover, and Xania Harrex for typing the poem inspired
by the painting;

the editors of *Span* in which 'Stiff Nor' Easter Across the Derwent'
and four other poems in this book were first published;

Jane for her 'Leda and the Swan' sketch and Jaime for his
little child's image, 'a poem in a bowl'.

I also gratefully acknowledge the following sponsors:

The Boating Industry Association
of South Australia and
General Manager, Glen Jones

Wirra Wirra Wines and
Chairman of Directors, Greg Trott

and Flinders University of South Australia, for supporting publication
of this book.

ALSO BY SYD HARREX

Atlantis and Other Islands
Inside Out
Dedications
No Worries, No Illusions, No Mercy

for Kiwi mates

Ken and Vince

Stiff Nor' Easter Across the Derwent*

In Memoriam David Harrex
2.6.1929 – 31.12.2001

O wild West Wind, thou breath of Autumn's being,
Thou, from whose unseen presence the leaves dead
Are driven, like ghosts from an enchanter fleeing,

Yellow, and black, and pale, and hectic red …
                                        —Shelley

Reading the wind, your eyes are treading
over and over across your home turf,
your childhood's mist-singing hills and seas;

those near and distant vicinities
your fingers read by sifting light from shade,
darkness from reflections in mirrors

no matter whether you are stuck in dunes,
or espying from a peak, or sketching
Balmoral Road ducks along Brown's River

as if to say each ink stroke or brush smudge
is a syllable or word, a wisp of sound,
shimmer of a hush, in a painted poem:

the water-colourist's language of precision.
See what the black rain gift reveals about
lightning and thunder, truth and deception;

fathom the intimate spaces you cover
and uncover inside the frame with the heart-
step tools of trade of the long-distance lover;

ecstatic now as your stiff nor' easter
sows tumult, skiffing on white caps to Storm Bay
in a climax of all your red-hectic energy.

But the aftermath is there as well, your
signature's skeleton in the south-east
corner, the serenity of a final calm
as you release the brush and rest your arm.

*Title of a watercolour by David Harrex which was awarded the
Australian American Association Maritime Art Prize 1990;
the painting is reproduced on the back cover*

Home Town

for Brian Levis 17.1.2001

It looked like Harry licking an ice-cream
cone-stepping up-town from the deep harbour
past the restaurant where I had scallops
for lunch with a semillon-chardonnay.
Haven't seen Harry, maybe, for twenty years.
Boy, how memory abbreviates time.
The past, what a prism; how stratified
the mind's history. Geological
layer-cake. Garbage bin of cliché
metaphors. But does Harry look okay!
Still got that Jesus look, though. Remember
when he built himself those rainbow wings,
climbed the sandstone wall and scaled the slate
roof of the church on Battery Point, clutched
the spire and prepared to sail like a kite
and land in Spoon Cove's shallow sea-water?
Boy, they don't allow inspired ones to be
so marvellously mad these days, do they?
But sure was him, know it in my bones, last
survivor from our free-fall angel time,
striding up-street normal as an ice-cream.
Going somewhere with purpose, like a law
of after life, muttering, 'to be sure, to be sure'.

About Islands

There where dodge tide tempests strafe the stubborn
girth of cliffs, flute fractured, earth disappears
so slowly only a life-time detects
the difference, and yet these vernaculars
of destruction—nouns bashed beyond recall,
verbs sliced by holocaust waves, crushed shells
of adjectives—only glass-mask the eyes
of the beachcomber who re-invents each
morning the grammar of the sea, footsteps
in quick damp sand, tablecloth imprints of fog
and dew grass where despair fluctuates
when the going gets tough until a hut,
simple on the sawed horizon, beside
a highland stream to nozzle in your throat,
beckons you in another direction
towards the island of an inland lake,
the deflections of glassed-in surrenders
the oceans of carnage hunger to destroy.
Here the territories of the starlight
are near as infinity ever gets,
the last of our final destinations.
Although life is a bitch, bloody mess,
death in the afternoon does not deny
the illumination of a coy mistress.
New legends spasm in the greening grass.

Growing into a New Age

The days and nights are shorter
being longer, hotter being colder.
I imagine grey-beard Archimedes
inventing a Principle for just these
circumstances when the speed
of autumn falling in its leafage
accelerates in contrary disposition
to the sloth with which limb and bone
attempt to stick-walk along a damp forest
floor, breath puffed out of an omega
mouth like the ashen tar of yester-
year's pack of twenty fags. Recall,
as I recall, the first cigar from a box
I bought in Havana. (Smoked it in front
of the photo exhibit, at the pier,
of Castro and Hemingway shaking hands,
as if some big shark's heart was being
squeezed; sharing their brotherhood …
but that's another story.) And my last
inhaled, exhaled, for twenty euphoric
minutes after dinner, on our deck,
its signals disappearing into a canopy
of summer stars, thousands already dead.

Solstice Hour-Glass

The season of retreating light
is upon us. Fog camouflages
the box shapes of houses.
Coffin-carriages are horse-drawn
through leather-bound chronicles,
their titles blurred on oak shelves
in the corners of a room of shadows.
There's a palpitation of silken
stealth, the trap-door spider
spinning a web out of the spine
of *Ancient Greek Myths and Legends.*
I open at random my winter
dictionary of astringent winds
in storm stricken trees, of sodden
pyre fuel smothered by an excess
of greenness, and am tongue-tied by
Todesgesang, Totengesang, 'various
insects making a sound like a watch
ticking', and *Todeswunsch* … a whisper
scattering of deathling letters, winged flocks
like agitated tea-leaves on the sky's page
or chisel-trapped in polished granite,
while mortal feet negotiate gravel:
this stuff our passovers are made of,
the atomic matter of our love.

The Other Night

The tenacious grain of elegy
impregnating solitude
like a fingerprint of finite flesh
leaves us choking on lack of breath.
There is no way of spelling
the spirit of that word, *death;*
neither as sense nor sound.

Where do we go from here?
Which doors do we lock and shut?
Which windows black out or open?
For something has to be ajar
and function like a lung
and let the sunlight in
as if for the first time again,

just as you turn your head
on your pillow in your moonlit sleep
at one with star-delight and dread.

Seeing is Knowing

You look at a blister of dew
on a blade of grass—remember
the Invisible Man's footprints
in the frost on the way to weatherboard
school rooms?—and you have to wonder
why you have the responsibility
of growing up and becoming an adult
in a world of family histories;
of sheets and pillows on the backyard line
and the sun and winds scouring the linen
of their secrets of forbidden knowledge
and the good Lord winking back at you
from the sun's eye in a dew blister
on a blade of glass which only
an insect's alert attention would know
was there, not worried by why, knowing why.

A Family Arrangement

My father and I seemed not to ask
each other questions that mattered.

It was an unspoken family arrangement
in which tokens of love and sentiment

were not for saying aloud. But when
it came to asking for a bus fare

and a one-pound note to see me through
he never faltered nor questioned whether

the need was my pedigree of weakness
or his sacrificial strength of recompense.

He simply gave and, silently, gave again,
weekly all the way to the yearly grave.

Child with Scissors

From my aerial view
above the galley bar
it's a field of wind-switched grass
he sits in—our Greek rug
piled from mountain wool
his busy blood keeps warm
as he snips cut-outs
to make his own book of life
from glossy magazines.

this is a jellyfish
with tentacles
see my lady I made
she's called Jube
he says, and offers up
a jagged fragment
of creation, of

his labour of unmaking
symmetrical neon pages
and flawless portraitures
flame-scissored into awkward stars
and ordinary creatures:

Protean, capricious; a world of delight
I recognise as roughly right.

The Precious Thing

I heard him say 'I've lost it'
and being but a small child—
for I was affectionately attached
to him—I wondered anxiously
what it was he lost. His cigarette
lighter perhaps, his wallet thin
with poverty but fat with black
and white photographs. Or his smile
which was of the trickster gentle kind.
So being an innocent I went
looking in the garden, down the street,
by the river, across the foot bridge, searching
for the precious thing he had lost
because of a bad-luck accident.
But all I found was a rabbit
palpitating in a trap, its leg
askew and leaking dark blood.
With all my puny strength, I freed
it, cradled it, avoiding its stare
so hypnotising and so like my
ancient uncle's who had lost
something I had gone looking for.
'Look', I said, giving him my
tender precious burden of pain
to hold and make better with
his healing hands. 'Ah, you found
it', he whispered, stroking the fur,
'my lucky charm, my rabbit's foot
I always keep in my trouser pocket,
but lost somewhere yesterday long ago.'

Fruits Instead of Flowers

In Memory of Lauris Edmond

'Fruits instead of flowers', you said
when last we spoke.
                              You were an expert
at tucking into bed the demanding
villanelle's rhymes and stanzas,
its courteous and wicked refrains,

like a dinner host pouring each glass
at the right taste-bud moment.

Always the children of your heart
anticipated the pure trance of art,
yet your muse was never weary. Two

lines of yours chandelier the candlelight
as we raise crystal goblets to your flame:
On sinful days and nights red wine is right
The wine of absolution is always white.

Impelled by the White Moon

for Peter Doley

Yes, I know we have talked about the blue
eyes, infatuation with the girl with black
hair slumbering under the orange tree

but I reassure you, she's no relation
of mine. I won't be offended if you bed
her under the stars in the old mateship

Australian way, or if you dive with her
in the naked moonlight in a rock pool
discreetly secreted in the Flinders Ranges.

Don't be surprised though, if you're woken
by sulphur-crested cockatoos shrieking
the death of the sperm's spiritual silence.

(How do you put it, the discipline of moss
like a creaking of the bones in galaxies
detected millions of light years later

like ashes in the dark corridors of dreams?):
those silent, static, alternatives to heartbeats
as you walk through my doorway, your scarf

trailing words I almost remember …
plague me no longer now, scarlet your
scarf, *for I am listening like the orange tree.*

Under a Medlar Tree

Madrigal of Maidenhead:
that's a fair thought to flower
under a medlar tree
where insect seconds eternalise
the hour and lovers commingling hair
find all the silken pleasures there,
their bodies rhyming like hammock couplets
in Shakespeare's summer sonnets.
Let us, too, rejuvenate those old arts
of passion that transcend night and day,
while muskets in the orchard spurt away
the beasts of envy and the birds of prey.

The Rain it Raineth Every Day

Tonight we are less complacent
torrents have been tormenting
drains are ceasing to sluice
rationality is losing its syntax

Tonight we are not what we were
a stupid way of admitting
the difference between a truth
and a lie as the crow flies

The wisdom of *that way madness
lies* is falling into smithereens
of rain that arranges its own
concerto patterns—stop-start heartbeats …

So be yourself … once insignificant
now a chiseller of messages
on headstones (a dying art you say)
but a decent way of making a living

And that's how death should be
the past nurturing the future
worms resurrecting the best ideas
butterflies fluttering out of novels

Heavens glossed with clouds, skies dissolving…

Inexorable C Minor

Twin sticks slowly syncopate
bone-jointed slaves
of brain hemispheres

this old man now who marches
with crease precision
in dry-cleaned trousers

his face scored, affaired
with musicological plots
still to be manuscripted

eyes spitting nails
into the coffin's last resort
anonymous silent crescendo.

A Vase of Wild Daffodils

something far more deeply interfused
—Wordsworth

You picked them a month ago and
despite the skittish tortoise-shell cat
vibrating with intimations of Spring
they have not been havocked yet, nor knocked
off their tea-tray table on wheels.
But let's face it, they are looking
wrinkled, they are whiskering
a sort of rot on the white
lace periphery of egg-yolk visages,
just as I imagine Dorothy
and William were prone to, towards
the close, blinking at elegiac sunset
light while echoes of a sense sublime
shiver like rain along the hills,
and heartbeats droop to rest in the dales,
and next season's daffodils slyly
prepare to bloom out of this year's slime.

Late Afternoon Light
Over the Lake

Across the lake's surface skin, warblers
upon the exfoliating clouds percussion
their own reflections of echoed sounds.

A cross-cut saw of raucousness
from crows in witches' attire
appears to endorse the Thane of Cawdor;

to show how endemic, even in nature—
and despite civilities of lawns, the
sedate gorgeousness of rose gardens—

are the gross barbecue ambitions
of bearded egos serving self first
while erasing the fifth commandment.

Pages of a newspaper, smudged scraps
of headline atrocities, hover
like sordid incense above rubbish bags

embellishing the lake's sedged edges.
Have we not learnt the difference
between the reflections and deceptions of water

as we sit here hearing our minds grinding,
while the birds swoop in and out with brains
in their beaks like writhing remnants of worms?

Maya

An empty chair
in the silent corridor

there are name-plates
on the polished doors

a door opens and lets
the wet darkness out

a cleaner removes
all traces of footprints

there's no evidence
the chair had been sat upon

the chair collapses
into thin air

the corridor haunted
by the hands of talk

swallows all its tongues;
walls, floors, rooms disappear.

Conundrums

That other dent in the pillow.
Passport Control at Mumbai.
Movable toilets after midnight.
How can the Infinite be split?
Massacres inside a golden temple.
Lip-stick kisses on an iceberg.
Today's death notices upside-down.
Knives and forks for left-handers.
Nightingale song inside the white pointer.
A four-letter word on the Cross.
Empty railway stations outside Eternity.
A dictionary arranged from Z to A.
Candlelight dripping on the missing page.
A lost match for the last candle.
The cosmos: full-stops that never end …

Belated Birthday Lunch

for Trevor

I have four lines of a song
that have sung themselves
into my winter head. I want
to write them down before
they vanish in the manner
of the best of dreams, but—
the eternal *but*—of the transient
universe intervenes, deracinates,
disfigures my costumed stances.

I wanted to write the lyrics down,
watch them integrate into dances,
but there's an interruption to respect,
a discussion to enter into with a friend
that is far more pressing than
your song's or mine's becoming.
Once the egg is broken in the mind
there is no time for distraction
if the omelette is to decorate the plate.

I had four lines of a song
but they are nowhere to be seen;
there was also a line or two
with an echo of 'nothing like the sun',
yet not deliberately obscene.
But happily I let them drift away
like cosmonauts whose life-lines are cut,
for this was your delayed birthday
and there were other things to think and say.

Dieter at the Wheel

Waves are nothing but water. So is the sea.
      — Sri Atmananda Guru
(frontispiece, Raja Rao, *The Serpent and the Rope*, 1960)

Doesn't the world revolve like a magic wheel?
Isn't Brahman the hub?
      — *The Bhagavadgita*
transcreated by P. Lal, 1965

India brought us together
but we never met there
—that's India. We met
in its hearsay meta-spaces
in Frankfurt and other
planetary places, and heard
the sounds of the Arabian
and Bengal Seas, the Indian
Ocean in each other's eyes.

That's the foreign gist
of my festschrift homage, mate,
Kumpel, Junge, and to elaborate:
Mensch, Bursche (notice my initials
enamelled in the supra text).

But, of course, this rhetoric
of reminiscence feebly awaits
transcreation into tropes of flame and snow
that correspond to the coastal music
of Malayalam, the pinnacles
of Sanskrit, and OM tissue-layered.

I see a book, an Orient Paperback
(I swear it's Anand's *Untouchable*)
open in your upright hands,
paragraphs poised between East and West,
and I see the bleeding soul
of the text bring a frown to your heart
and anguish to your tongue:

                      'how
can such injustice be tolerated
by this society so admired
for its toleration?' And there
we have it: the paradox trap,
conundrum clouds in *maya* sky.
Matter of spirit, spirit of matter.

And before we know it, philosophy
hangs like meat in the metaphysicians'
butcher shop, and though we escape
to drown our hermeneutical sorrows
in *Bitburger Pils,* the fact remains
that the infamous game of dice
was not the right solution, yet without
it the long-run of the epic would not
have secured victory in the long run.

So what do we see in the super myth's wake?
— War that fails to fail, rife with secondaries
as the surgeon says, imploding our
pock-marked globe trapped by
a sun, the Wheel of Life, programmed
to explode eternities before
infinity itself …

                  Hence we share ideas,
knowing consolation must be stoical,
and that our minds are, perhaps miraculously,
too small and too large to contain
waves that are nothing but water.

Meanwhile, I don't see you now in a dhoti
in your new ashrama of Retirement,
but rather (voyeur-wise) I detect
sarong shapes on your washing-line
on a Pakeha Tasman ledge down under:

the salt syllables of a sacred song
echoing in the mouth of the Roaring Forties.

Aachen, Germany, 31.5–1.6.2000

Ford Juggernaut

I see a truck
with a bold sign
painted on it

ALL STATES
REMOVALS

and say to myself
what a good idea.

A Lover's Anguish in King William Street

A Doctor of Baltic Studies
wondering where his next
overseas grant was coming from

stopped at the red light
& glancing at the sun-blocking
vehicle in the right-hand lane

saw this sign on the truck's
left-side indented panel:
HORIZONTAL BORING SPECIALISTS

which even in Adelaide's
Queen Victoria Square
is still capable of exciting

the genitalia of exhausted angels.

Where are the Toilets?

Panic, panic. The Memorandum says
(flushing my imagination), 'Please find
attached EMERGENCY EVACUATION
PROCEDURES'. My eyes boggle at that.
What does the document consist of?—rolls
of inscribed toilet paper snailing up
and down the corridors? But worse to come:
'The text must be read out at commencing [*sic*]
lectures each year'. But there are no directions,
no maps, displaying toilet locations
near or far in case of chilli and spice
curry emergencies during the 2.00–2.50 pm
lecture, and not even one iota's note
from Counselling about anal retentive
learning disorders. Memo ends, 'Thank you
for your cooperation in this matter.'

Notes about Inertia

Instead of drowning
in a desirable congestion
of estuary tides

consider the illusion
of floating like a raft;
bubbles of certified

carefree indolence
issuing from your mouth
without due responsibility.

But weather of one season
or another is inescapable,
inside either the sleeping head

or sleep's dreaming pillow.
The psyche's magnifying glass
will never let you forget

the almost invisible scars,
especially the self-inflicted
most recurrent one which shows

to your faces in disguise
what a hypocrite you are.
Yet not even this confession

rising like morning mist
from a mirror-futile lake
can excuse your lassitude.

Every attempt to smoke-screen
forbidden fruit of memory
is a camouflage for despair.

Old props of emptiness
litter the cellar café table:
the wine-vacant glasses

stained with second-hand sunsets,
the ash-tray crematorium,
the stale scent of Gauloise Bleu;

those sauce-smeared napkins
surrendering a final imagery
of the beauty of roses, crumpled.

In the Doctor's Waiting Room

for Tim Moss

Not often, I admit, but sometimes you
can watch the moss grow on the artificial
stones around the flowers in the waiting room—
those icons of serenity and optimism
designed to fantasise the idea that
your body doesn't really play nasty
tricks at your expense. Believe that subliminal
advertising and you will trust anyone.
From media magnate to Minister of the Crown,
from bureaucrats to talk-back radio shockjocks;
the list is a continuum of ice
in the heart of humanism. But enough
of that ad nauseam cancer in the system.
Back in the waiting room (admirably
named, no false advertising, Kafka's novels
are full of these indefinitely claustrophobic
spaces); as I was saying, back to the doc's
waiting room which you should enter in slippers
sanitised for the occasion, where a casually
terse nervous silence prevails, so much so
the difference between an unforced cough
and a congealed whisper is almost in-
audible. Patients magnetised to their chairs
flick the shiny pages of magazines
they are unaccustomed to reading. Their hooded
eyes unroll random phrases like lottery
marbles, words like *colostomy irrigation,*
urinary tract infection, bargain basement *hospice,*
skeletal tractions, endometrial hyperplasia.
But at least the vitamin D sun streams
through the antiseptic windows on the seaward
side, and the flowers in the vases next to
the safe sex brochures are illuminatingly
tactile (until you touch them and feel plastic silk),
like aromatic condoms stretched to the limit
during a one-night stand in a hotel suite
which looks uncannily like a doctor's surgery.

Burial

How the things that seem to touch you least
can hurt the most, how the elegy lingers.
Like our cat's fur between my fingers, as I
prepare to carry her in a sling of a blanket,
sunset-faded pink, perforated by mice,
to the grave I have just been digging.
I know this is a truly family event,
and heart-juggling, when body contradicts
the soul, and maggot eaten-out the mouth
and crow-plundered the eyes, the jugular wounds,
are belied by dreaming tortoiseshell beauty
sleeping in the sheltering grass under
an olive tree.
        And so it is we're reminded
that every death-drifting phrase must rest
somewhere, a hillside perhaps, where the grief
cannot quantify either the pleasure or the pain
and the mind is a trap-door to an undefined
elsewhere, or otherwise, or distant nebula.
Neither letting in nor out the very word
that is unsaid by being said
summoning the living, comforting the dead.

Four Haikus

A black and white storm
punched an umbrella dome
crimson in the rain.

Euclid and Newton
showed there was more to apples
than lust in Eden.

Like a Chinese scroll
the willow of Lara's bat
unfolds boundaries.

Watch Li Po, friends, flex
his kite's finger string, and palm
poems out of skies.

In a Japanese Garden

for Karen

Stroll in from the sun.
Camouflage of leaves
pasted together will shade

you. There are grasses
like combed hair, petal
ponds & carved shrubs.

Be detached from service
to East-West dialogue
& resume your *self*.

A fish flaps
into air & for
the instant skis
on its tail,

just like a haiku.

Here is a fair place
for smiles to flower:
green sphere for memory
to let in scents of wattle;
venue of farewells
beside the toy waterfalls,
the miniature steps,
of Japanese eternity …

Face Lifts

East-West Center, Honolulu

1
She sketches faces
round the conference table.
What would happen
I wonder if someone else
sketched her sketching
someone else, and
everyone at the table
practised the same discipline?

Like the insoluble problem
at my childhood breakfasts
of Infinity disappearing
into a cereal packet.

2
Tact is not his forté.
He is too honest
to be humble.

Pacific Romantic
living in a high
fidelity cave,
he invites himself
to a Maori's house
to apologise
for inviting himself
to a Maori's house.

He leaves with a new image
for his non-stop poem.

3
Call her the Dowager.
Picture her on a chaise-longue
in the middle of the room
(let Goya come to mind)
as the women come and go
and the men (one intoning
'the best poets steal'),
the men kneel.

Dispensing gifts of wit
and long-suffering advice
to Korea/Malaysia/Sri
Lanka/India/Bangladesh/
New Zealand/&/Australia.

The Reclining Nude
of American Poetry.

4.
Sometimes I think he smokes
only to cough,
coughs just to smoke.

Is it because
without tobacco
he can't unlatch
the garden gate
of flower-cyphered song
the scrolled night long?

or because he's candidly
waiting (erect amid clouds,
sulphuric sunlight)
to become
                an extinct
                        VOLCANO?

5
Headmistress huntress
of skulls, of errant sea-shelled
brains, she should have been:
an apposite vocation.

I see her seated
at a Dickensian desk
red-ruling the ledgers of love;
disappointed (of course)
with delinquent blood,
Pakeha poison;

her cane inflaming the knuckles
of fickle legends.

By mere stroking
of the anxious waves, she
hauls in a rainbow net
of fish: an applause
of salted praise—
of mackerel, herring,
perch, white-bait especially,
and even claws, claws
clapping their applause.

6
That horizon cloud
is daughter to Kazuko
whose eyes are raining.

7

This is a generous man,
a deceptively decisive man.
Below his tufted brows
slow eyes are good for finding
again hospitable huts
on painted Chinese mountains.
Some there are who learn from this,
the calligraphy of steps
descending to a pool,
each slab a tone segment,
each segment a shape, each shape
a sedge of sound:

           as if heartbeats
are footsteps in packed snow
and footfall Death only a shadow
sunlight suffers in order to let go.

Couple in a Courtyard

They hold each other as if their bond
is an empty bag of sweets.
He cannot speak the words
that would fail him anyway.
Her eyes above his shoulder
stare out of a winter-famished face
beyond his black shore of hair
into the vortex of a wind that rips
all vulnerable shapes in sight,
anything that will bend and break.

Sitting for a Portrait

The greying man is sitting silently.
His deck-chair fronts the sea. The eyes
stare as if he's looking nowhere you
or I, painter or witness, can identify.
A scarf is twirled around his throat
like an old-school rainbow drab and faded.
If he wriggles at all, no one notices.
Expectant sea-birds, acquisitive, competitive,
are beaks in waiting. There are signs
the sitter's lunch is about to be served:
fish might be too much to expect, but crusts
are acceptable to predators; even the last
crumbs, devoured quickly one by one.

Leda and the Swan:
A Stone Carving and a
Felt-Pen Sketch

I wonder if Yeats ever happened on
it: a relief of Leda and the Swan
intact in a frieze fragment of sweet stone;
sweet, I mean, with sand-flesh grain, chiselled tone.
It's in a dim museum ante-room
which grim guards sometimes open, like a tomb.
Overlooked by decadent Roman busts
so cut as to fashion the real men's lusts
astride the power ethic, Zeus's rape
of Leda (the swan's beak prising her nape,
legs positioning for the lava thrust)
sleeps like history's shadow in the dust.

I asked an artist to draw it for me,
wondering what the sex in her would see.
I have her troubled sketch before me now:
the swan's neck tautened like a cord-strung bough,
the outstretched wings a god's gross appetite,
the feathers like reptile scales; the swan's might
tremouring towards a bloody embrace …
the strange concentration on Leda's face,
as she strains, hand between her thighs, to aid
the act, knowing gods are of woman made.
This both sketch and carving show: carnal pride,
old sorrows, because of which love has died.

Judy's Angel

You adore this orchardist's angel
dappled and sculpturesque in autumn.

Melbourne girl model whose story
will never be revealed. But she

is no anorexic: see her sumptuous
contours and prize certainty in her eyes;

this pose in lift-off evangelation,
the left wing blood-floodingly uplifting.

And what I take that you take to be
the one staggering shuddering moment

when she swells on the rippling waters
walking across the sky's reflections.

Occasionally, just one stone image
never seems to decay, never seems to lie.

Late Afternoon, Granite Island

I hadn't realised before how grey greyness is,
that most boring, uninspiring of colours
outside the rainbow spectrum; much maligned
and totally neglected as a source of beauty.
But here, now, grey infuses everything: the light
that wants to be milky, the sea that wants
to be the coat of many colours, the sky
that wants the credit for everything
(beautiful moon, mystical sun, enchanting
stars ascendant), the hills that want to be green,
the rocks ochre, the ripples crystal-glinting.
Yet I take heart from the majestic endorsement
of the jetty whose wood has greyed to total greyness,
while generations have sulked and cried spilt
milk, and does its job as it always has,
supporting departures and arrivals greyly
in a black and white movie as time goes by.

Shoeless Evenings

for Vincent Megaw

He promenades now, back less vertical
than I remember ... (those shoeless sunsets,
& paddling ampersand footprints, & this
phosphorescent tug and incandescent sigh
of wetness, dryness; of passion integral;
of the moon's gravitational pull
magnetically doing the colour-in
bits of these Clifford Possums in damp sand).

Does that signify he's not immortal?
or is this just one more fondling foolish
question that disguises the true presence
of spies in our dreams where tears and laughter
swap places, like twins in the Renaissance
bard's ingenious comic-sumptuous plot?

Errors are his forté. Without them, he asks,
how to determine scientifically
the fate of a bone in an ancient pit
with a mantra of forensic patience;
the sacred rage or lust? Or is the bone's
echo of despair corporeal too
with the mute gusto grit of tenderness?

Our questioner walks, toes dug in, upright
to the end of the strand. A froth of gulls
career, squabbling, out of the ocean mist
while a musical score—I think the Handel
Fireworks extravaganza—saturates his soul.

Chopping Wood

It was once a gully for grazing cattle,
these idle pastures adjoining
yet another parish of brick suburbia …

I select a stump that's boneish grey
like some giant's thigh bogged
here by mistake and now half
grown over with spike and leaf
of blackberry shoots.
When with arc'd axe I hack
its once rock-tough wood,
how easily its shell fissures,
and how ingratiatingly new-made
soil spills out like stuffing
from a doll decapitated.

Ants white as well as black,
Time's accessaries, have done their work
tunnelling veins of sap,
returning blood to earth.
I chop and split thinking of tonight's
steaks sizzling above white-hot coals;
how the human sum of satisfactions
depends on carcasses of cow and tree
and such ephemera in summer
pastures shaded by vast gums where,
today at least, Golden Hawks safely nest.

Call it Love

Putting your life on the line:
you pretend not to watch the magpies
every morning eating away sleep
like scattered biscuits and cheese.
You put it on the clothesline, short of pegs,
because you want to show your true colours
to the wind. Truly simple-minded, you
want the world to be a better place;
you want those bruised-peach breezes to visit
the ancestral furniture of darkened
forebears. You want the estuary moon
to contemplate other circumferences in
the universe. And, below all, you want
the aurora of the first kiss at sun-blinked night
to be the evermore. You know what it means,
despite the raven wings: call it love.

Some Take Wing Sooner Than Others

In Memoriam Richard Conyers

'I would like these lines
to be as elastic as lilies',
Ezra Pound once almost said.

Their blood-line transience implies
old conspiracies of canals, Venetian
of course, flickering over facades

in ornate apertures of palaces
waxed by the shroud-shutting
and dream-opening of bygone eyes.

Suppose things had been different:
locked doors ajar, someone gone
replacing someone here. Perhaps

only the living and the dead
(whose grandfathers often wore
gloves, magician white, above

the graveside) share more intimate
illuminations than ourselves can ever
apprehend, garlanded here.

Nothing less complicated
than severing of leaf from twig,
of bedside grief from gradual death

can transubstantiate the roses
aflame on the coffin's breast, nor
chrysanthemums breathing like fish;

fragrancing the dusk with wisps and motes
of mortal music, words unworded
in the sandstone of brittle sermons;

nor can ghosts in quiescent mist
distance suspicion of presence (that
intimate insect in the eyelashes)

from this face there at the window
which fades as it brightens recollection
while seagulls interrupt the sleep of air.

5–6.9.2000

LYTHRUM

LYTHRUM PRESS PTY LTD
1st floor, 128 Hindley Street
Adelaide
South Australia 5000

Telephone: (08) 8415 5150

www.lythrumpress.com.au